LIVING A[illegible]
CHALLENC[illegible]

***"By understanding [illegible]
with GOD"***

Prince .A. Onyechere

Living above the challenges of life.

"By Understanding the power of unity with God"

I.S.B.N. NO: 9780993130892

Published by: Graceland Book Publishers United Kingdom

Tel United kingdom: +447909489415

Unless otherwise indicated, all Scripture quotations are taken from The King James version of the Holy Bible.

Printed in the United Kingdom

FORWARD

Any man, who makes himself a friend of God, becomes a master of the challenges of life. A man with a winning attitude and faith in God becomes the master of the circumstances of life. Life is filled with circumstances that are very challenging to man and unless a man aligns himself with his creator he will definitely experience defeat in the battle of life. The scripture makes us to understand that "Nay in all these things we are more than conquerors through Christ Jesus". We are to emulate the heroes of faith in the bible, who our Lord used to teach us how to become the masters of the winds and storms of life. The author goes through the scriptures to teach us about life and the challenges that the heroes of faith faced but overcame because they had absolute trust in God. His personal challenge of having to see his daughter crippled, but miraculously healed proves that he is not only a man writing from personal experiences, but he is also a man with an in depth knowledge of the word of God and how to be a master to the challenges of life. To become a master to the storms of life we must have that kind of faith that our Lord demonstrated to his disciples while he walked on the sea. Through the storms of life we are able to prove to the world that the master walks with us at all times to make us champions and masters to the challenges of life. This book is a about becoming a master to the challenges of life by using the authority of the believer and the biblical principles of faith, hope and patience. This book is recommended to all lovers of good books.

Pastor Chinyere.D .Nwakanma

London United Kingdom

INTRODUCTION

Whenever you are in distress, all you need to do is to turn to the Lord, seek Him and you will find him. Don't just sit down feeling helpless. Your needs for comfort and God's supply of comfort are always in perfect balance because he wants to meet you at the point of your every need.

God has a shepherd's heart. You are His weak lamb, discouraged and beaten but carried in his arms. Since God is your ultimate comforter, His words are your greatest source of comfort. God's word is as close to you, as your fingertips, and God is as close to you as your whispered prayer.

One crucial point from the story of the city of Smyrna was how a city in ruins turned into a beautiful city three hundred years later.

A remarkable lesson from the story of this city was the sacrificial killing of Polycarp, the Bishop of Smyrna.

The Jews in Smyrna were quite hostile to the church when Polycarp was eighty some persecutors surrounded him and tied him to a stake, ready to set him on fire. He was to be spared only if he recanted his faith and denied Christ. However, he replied that if the Lord had been faithful to him for the past eighty years, why would he deny Him now? In their fury, they set him ablaze, but he was not burnt. Then in anger a soldier stabbed him and he bled until the fire around him was quenched by his blood. He became one of the earliest Martyrs who died for Jesus Christ and his death strengthened the faith of others. With modernization and technological advancement, it has become more and more difficult for believers to put their lives on the line because of God's word.

But will we allow technological developments and civilization to erode our faith in Jesus Christ? The sophistication in Smyrna did not stop believers from being committed to the Lord until death. The less committed you are to Christ, the more the chances that Satan, the world and flesh will devour you.

Do you love Jesus Christ to the point of dying because of him? Do you have the ability to stand hunger, humiliation, joblessness, demotion and intense persecution, because of your faith in Jesus Christ? As you read this book, may the Lord grant you the grace to stand in times when your faith in Jesus Christ is being challenged?

NUGGETS OF WISDOM

- You do not fail if you don't give up. You only fail when you give up ---- Mike Murdock.
- Limitations live only in our minds, but if we use our imaginations, our possibilities becomes limitless -----Jamie Paolinetti.
- Some men are born mediocre, some men achieve mediocrity and some men have mediocrity thrust upon them ------Joseph Heller.
- Life is like riding a bicycle. To keep your balance, you must keep moving --- Albert Einstein.
- Always bear in mind that your own resolution to succeed is more important than any other ------Abraham Lincoln
- All Progress is precarious, and the solution of one problem brings us face to face with another problem ------- Martin Luther King Jnr.

CONTENTS

CHAPTER ONE

The Power of Patience

In Samuel 1:1, we read about Hannah, and her tribulations. Firstly, she lived at a terrible time in the history of Israel. The troubled nation was merely a loose confederacy of tribes, united only by the worship of Jehovah at the shrine in Shiloh. Invaders harassed Israel year after year, with strong leaders called judges ruling the people, but only to find the Israelites oppressed by different groups of invaders.

Not only was Hannah's nation oppressed by their neighbours, but the religious life of the people was corrupted by bad priests who sometimes derail from the service of God, leading the people to sin by serving other gods. It was not a time that faith and devotion to God was being inspired in Israel.

Yet, in the midst of this religious hypocrisy we find a pious family living in Ramah in the hill country allotted to the tribe of Ephraim. Elkanah, the man of the house was a Levite or a priest. Every year Elkanah and his family made the ten mile journey on foot to the tabernacle or shrine at Shiloh to worship.

Hannah lived at a stressful time both politically and religiously. But she also had to live with the problems in her family. In 1Samuel 1:2, we learnt that Elkanah had two wives -Hannah, who was more loved but barren and Peninnah, who was less loved but was very fertile. Some of Hannah's problems came as a result of her being in a polygamous marriage.

In Hannah's case it was likely that she was Elkanah's first wife. But because she was infertile, he took a second wife to insure that the family name would not be lost because he had no children.

In Hannah's times, a woman who failed to produce children was considered to be irrelevant to the accomplishment of the Messianic promise. Hannah's situation was very depressing. Year after year Peninnah gave birth to children; year after year Hannah suffered emotional abuse from her rival, as a result of her infertility, her hopes for pregnancy receding with every menstrual period. Hannah's problems in the family could be attributed to being in a polygamous marriage and from her infertility as she lived next to a co-wife who had no problem conceiving and bearing children.

Hannah's problems however were compounded by the fact that Peninnah never stopped taunting her about her childlessness, it was understood that her rival Peninnah kept provoking her in order to irritate her and this had been going on for a long time year after year.

One of the most trying times of Hannah's life was during the annual pilgrimage to Shiloh. Imagine having to walk for ten miles with someone who never stopped picking at your inadequacies while her children kept bumping into you, wiping their noses on your skirt, or asking you to carry them. No wonder Hannah arrived at Shiloh under a black cloud of depression. The Scriptures says

> "My brethren, count it all joy when you fall into various trials. Knowing that the testing of your faith produces patience, but let patience have its perfect work that you may be perfect and complete, lacking nothing" (James 1:2-4).

In the midst of it all, however Hannah did not lose her grip of God, see what happened next;

> "Once when they had finished eating and drinking in Shiloh, Hannah stood up, now Eli the priest was sitting on a chair by the doorpost of the Lord's temple (tabernacle). From within her soul in bitterness Hannah wept much and prayed to the Lord".

Hannah has been suffering silently, very much like many women suffering today, but she did something else. She prayed to the Lord, the first time we heard her words was when she was addressing God;

> "She made a vow saying O Lord Almighty, if you will only look upon your servant's misery and remember me and not forget your servant but give her a son then, I will give him to the Lord for all the days of his life and no razor will ever be used on his head".

Hannah's vow was called a **Nazirite vow**. Read about Hannah as she asked God to give her a son. Feel her desperation and the urgency of her petition. "Look at my misery, remember me! Don't forget me! Give me a son!" We can feel the heaviness in the words as she prayed.

> "As she kept on praying to the Lord, Eli observed her mouth. Hannah prayed in her heart and her lips moved but her voice was not heard. Eli thought that she was drunk and said to her, "how long will you keep on getting drunk? Get rid of your wine. Not so my Lord, Hannah replied; I am a woman who is deeply troubled, I have not been drinking wine or beer, I was pouring out my soul to the Lord. Do not take your servant for a wicked woman, I have been praying here out of my great anguish and grief'.

Hannah had to deal with the unjustifiable criticisms from the one who misunderstood her, in addition to Peninnah's jibes. In the prayer, she made a vow that if the Lord gave her the desire of her heart, she would give that son back to him to serve him all the days of his life. But that vow and her pleas did not account for all the time Hannah stood and prayed. From within her soul, Hannah wept much and prayed and she kept on praying. This is called understanding the power of unity in action. No wonder Eli the priest asked her to go in peace and prayed the God of Israel to grant her what she had asked of him.

Notice this beloved; then Hannah went her way and ate something and her face was no longer downcast. Have you seen how understanding the power of unity with God worked in the life of this woman Hannah?

Hannah joined in the worship of the Lord, the next morning, she went back to Ramah with Elkanah, and Voila, before long she was pregnant and gave birth to Samuel whose name meant "heard of God". She asked God for a child and He heard her and answered her prayer; no wonder her problem was solved. She had the baby she asked for.

The key to understanding the dramatic turn-around in Hannah's life in verse eighteen lies in her song or psalm that could be found in 1 Samuel 2:1-10.

Hannah's problems were lifted when she took focus away from herself and her situation but focused on God in the midst of her misery then was she able to focus on the three important facts about God. She underlined these three facts in her song.

The first thing she knew about God was found in 1Samuel 2:2.

> "There is no one holy like the Lord there is no one besides you; there is no rock like our God".

She recognized God's holiness and what God's holiness meant to a woman in distress. Far from being consoling, that could only intensify the feelings of worthlessness and guilt that are often part of depression.

Holiness is not the mere absence of evil; it is also the presence of positive right. It is God at work doing what is positively right for us. His love is a holy and pure love that is committed to our best good.

The second thing Hannah knew about God was found in 1Samuel 2:3,

"For the Lord is a God who knows and by him deeds are weighed".

The New American standard bible translates thus; "for the Lord is a God of Knowledge". Not only does God's holiness keep him committed to our best good, his perfect knowledge keeps him from doing anything in our lives that is not perfectly right for us.

Someone has said that God does not waste his strokes in our lives. This is true; because God knows what the best is for us. There are no trials and error, no foul balls or strikeouts with God. God is a God of knowledge and we can have confidence that He is able to do what is right for us at all times. The third thing Hannah knew occupied much of her song. God has power; we see this in 1Samuel 2:6-7 and at the end of verse 8.

> "The Lord brings death and makes alive, he brings down to the grave and raises up. The Lord sends poverty and wealth, he humbles and he exalts.
>
> For the foundations of the earth are the Lord's, upon them he has set the world. The Lord of creation has all power. He can do whatever he wants to do".

This fact without the first two facts might terrify us, if God had all power and we did not know anything else about Him we do have massive problems. We would all cower in dark corners to escape his wrath or his caprice. But God tempers his power with his commitment to our welfare. He controls his power with his knowledge of what is the best for us at every point in time in our lives.

God is infinite, God is infallible, he wants what is best for us and knows with perfect knowledge what is best, and He also has the power to make the best things to happen in our lives. God's holy commitment to us works with His knowledge of what is best for us and God's power to make the right things happen in our lives are all linked together to our good.

What brought Hannah out of her problem was the fact that she saw God as He really was; this was as a result of her understanding of the power of unity with God through prayers.

Hannah's story had a happy ending. Samuel was born and she gave him to the Lord. God gave her three more sons and two daughters. Yes, in 1samuel 1:18, when she stopped praying, she ate some food and stopped looking sad, she didn't know at that moment how the story would end. She was able to do that because she had met with God and 'understood' who He was and what he could do.

Psychologists believe that failure is related to the way we think about ourselves. It is also true that it is related to the way we think or fail to think about God. Once we join ourselves to a Good-sized God, we have enough resources for dealing with failure or the problems of life.

We can focus on God, - His holiness, His knowledge and His power. We can face our fears and anxieties in the light of His character and His commitment to us.

If failure results from the way we think about ourselves, then it could be removed by the way we think about ourselves in relation to a holy, knowledgeable and powerful God who is committed to us. This could be made possible when we work in unity with Him. Accomplishing His will on planet earth as the scriptures say "let thy Kingdom come and your will be done."

Robert Browning reminded us that it is looking downwards that makes one dizzy. I am an acrophobia, I didn't like being up high on the top of things like fire towers or monuments or skyscrapers. Looking down terrifies me.

Spiritually speaking, the downward look is the one that leads to failure; the upward look takes away our fears. Look to the God of Hannah, the one who solved her problems with a new understanding which is His love, His knowledge and His Power.

CHAPTER TWO

The Power of having a close walk with God

Elisha was a Prophet of God anointed to carry on the ministry of Elijah after his demise. In 1 kings19:15-21 we read the story of the call of Elisha. God had instructed Elijah to anoint Elisha the son of Shaphat in his room.

Elisha was a farmer with twelve Oxen. He had family commitments and a business. His father and mother were worried and tried to stop him from answering the call of God that was upon his life. But he went on to serve his God .And some of the turning points in Elisha's life were these-

2 Kings 2:9, "Ask what I shall do for thee before I am taken away from thee.

Let a double portion of thy Spirit be upon me. Elisha replied.

"Thou has asked a hard thing nevertheless if thou see me when I would be taken from thee. And Elisha saw it, he cried my father, my father, the chariot of Israel, the horsemen and he took up also the mantle of Elijah that fell from heaven, with the mantle he performed the first miracle which is parting of River Jordan".

One of the most outstanding miracles Elisha did in his time was when the Israelites were at war with the Syrian army.

The king of Syria consulted his Army officers and chose a place to set up his camp in order to lay ambush against Israel. But Elisha sent words to the king of Israel, warning him to stay clear from the place, because the Syrians had laid ambush there, so the Israelites were on guard. This happened several times.

This incident provoked the king of Syria greatly as he called his officers and asked them, "Which one of you is exposing our secrets to the king of Israel". They answered no and made it clear to him that Prophet Elisha revealed secrets of nations to the kings of Israel. The king of Syria ordered his army officers to find out where Prophet Elisha was so as to capture him.

When the king of Syria was told that Elisha was in Dothan, he sent forces there with horses and chariots. They reached the town at night and surrounded it. Early the next morning Elisha's servant got up, went out of the house and saw the Syrian troops with their horses and chariots surrounding the town. He went back to Elisha and exclaimed "We are doomed, Sir; What shall we do?"

Elisha answered, "Do not be afraid, for those who are with us are more than those who are with them". Then Elisha prayed, O lord open his (Elisha's servant) eyes and let him see. The Lord answered his prayer and Elisha's servant looked up and saw the hill side covered with horses and chariots of fire all around Elisha.

When the Syrians army attacked, Elisha prayed, "O Lord strike these men blind". The Lord answered his prayer and struck them blind.

> "The Lord is my light and salvation whom shall I fear, the Lord is the strength of my life of whom shall I be afraid, When the wicked came against me to eat up my flesh my enemies and foes they stumbled and fell, though an army may encamp against me, my heart shall not fear; though war may rise against me; in this I will be confident; Psalms27:1-3"

Just notice the confidence that Elisha had in God .Elisha was not afraid of the Assyrian king and his mighty army. Elisha had a committed relationship with God as a result of his understanding of the power of unity with God.

The significance of the double portion of the anointing, as a result his relationship with God is very important in understanding how close Elisha was with God. Elisha had the understanding that it was the anointing that could give him everything that he needed as a servant of God. This showed that he was a man at unity with God. Elijah performed sixteen miracles whereas his servant Elisha performed thirty two miracles.

(THE MIRACLES ELISHA PERFORMED BY ELISHA):

1. Drying of the Jordan.	2kings 2:13-15
2. Healing of the Waters.	2kings 2:19
3. Bears coming from the wood.	2kings 2:23
4. Water filling ditches without rain	2kings 3:16-20
5. Defeat of the Moabites	2kings 3:18-24
6. Optical illusion	2kings 3:21-23
7. The Increase of the widow's oil	2kings 4:1-7
8. The Bareness was Healed	2kings 4:12-17
9. The Resurrection of a boy	2kings 4:32-37
10. Pottage Healed	2kings 4:28
11.Bread was multiplied for 100 men	2kings 4:42
12. Naaman the leper was healed	2kings 5:1-14
13.Discernment of Gehazi	2kings 5:23
14.Leprosy of Naaman given to Gehazi	2kings 5:27
15.Recovery of Axe head on water	2kings 6:1-7
16.Recovery of war secrets	2kings 6:10
17.Revealing the War Secret	2kings 6:13
18. Servants eyes opened	2kings 6:13
19.Blinding of the Syrian Army	2kings 6:13
20.Reviving war secrets	2kings 6:13
21.Capturing Syria Army	2kings 6:19

22.Healing the Syrian Armies blindness	2kings 6:20
23.Fire knowing the King's Act	2kings 6:32
24.Miraculous Utterances	2kings 7:1
25.Miraculous Utterances	2kings 7:2
26.Confusing the Syrian Army Camp	2kings 7:6-8
27.Seven years of famine	2kings 8:1-2
28.Miraculous Utterance s	2kings 8:7-11
29.Miraculous Utterance s	2kings 8:12
30.Miraculous Utterances	2kings 8:13-15
31.Miraculous Utterance s	2kings 9:1-10
32.Miraculous Utterance s	2kings 13:14-19

Conclusion: 1kings 19:21 tells us that Elisha rose and went after Elijah and ministered unto him. The lesson we are to learn from here is that even though God had called Elisha into the prophetic office, he had to answer that call. He had to sacrifice the comfort of his former life and be a servant of God

Secondly, he had to be trained to stand in the office of that ministry.

Thirdly, he had to be tested and proven to have the ability to function in that office. 2kings 2:1: And it came to pass when the Lord would take up Elijah into heaven by a whirlwind that Elijah went with Elisha from Gilgal.

So, we can see and understand that Elisha worked closely with Elijah before he started his prophetic ministry

This is called understanding the power of unity in action, which is a very important key to the transference of the anointing.

Three times Elijah did ask Elisha to stay back for the Lord had sent him to Bethel, Jericho, Jordan but Elisha's answer was "as the Lord liveth and as thy soul liveth I will not leave thee". Because he wanted to be close and united with his master.

Elisha received the double portion of the anointing that was upon Elijah as he desired.

CHAPTER THREE

The Power of Sacrificial Living

Shadrack, Meschack and Abednego were three young men who lived at a time when the Jews suffered great persecutions and oppressions from a pagan king .Shadrack, Meshach and Abednego were low paid workers of the Babylonian and Persian empires. They were foreigners who had powerful impacts on the government through being at the right place at the right time.

King Nebuchadnezzar made a gold statue which was ninety feet tall and nine feet wide and set it up on the plain of Guru in the province of Babylon.

He (King Nebuchadnezzer) called all the provincial officials including the princes, governors, advisors, counselors, judges, magistrates and prefects to come and witness the dedication of the statue (god) he had made.

When all these officials had arrived and stood before the image king Nebuchadnezzar had made, a herald shouted out. People from all races, nations and languages listened to the King's command that they must bow to the ground to worship the graven image. Anyone who refused the King's order must be thrown into a blazing furnace.

All the people of all races, nations and Languages, including all the officials bowed to the ground and worshiped the image (god) Nebuchadnezzar made.

But some people went to the King and informed him that Shadrack, Meschack and Abednego had refused to bow and worship the image (god) he had made. King Nebuchadnezzar could have imagined that he was the final authority in the whole kingdom and nobody could be contemptuous to his decrees. He did turn himself into a demi god. Nebuchadnezzar in his pride flew into a rage probably because he knew that Shadrack, Meshach and Abednego were small young men (Jews), commoners and slaves who served him. How could they reject his orders and refuse to obey him and he ordered his servants to bring Shadrach, Meshach and Abednego before him,

Nebuchadnezzar wanted to give Shadrack, Meshack and Abednego the last chance to defend and save themselves by compromising and bowing to his image, as well as to confirm the report of their accusers, King Nebuchadnezzar said to them "is it true, Shadrach, Meshach and Abednego that you refuse to serve my gods or to worship the gold image I have set up".

Nebuchadnezzar even went ahead by boasting that no other god can ever deliver Shadrack, Meshack and Abednego out of his power. Shadrack, Meshach and Abednego replied; "O Nebuchadnezzar, we have no need to answer you on this matter. If it be so, our God whom we serve is able to deliver us from the burning fire furnace and he will deliver us out of your hand. O king, but if not, be it known unto you, O King, that we will not serve your gods, nor worship the golden image which you have set up".

What a faithful word from these gentlemen who had purposed in their hearts that no matter the circumstances they find themselves in, that they will never serve or worship any other god except the almighty God. This is having an understanding of the power of unity with God in action.

"The Lord is on my side, I will not fear what man can do unto me. Psalm 118:6.

Who shall separate us from the love of Christ? Shall tribulation or distress, or persecution or famine or nakedness, or peril, or sword? It is written for your sake we are killed all the daylong, we are accounted as sheep for the slaughter, For I am persuaded, that neither death nor life nor angels nor principalities nor powers nor things to come, nor height, nor depth, nor any other creation, shall be able to separate us from the love of God, which is in Christ Jesus our Lord". Romans 8:35-36 &38-39.

King Nebuchadnezzar could not believe his ears, for no one has ever confronted and challenged him in that manner in the whole history of the kingdom.

Nebuchadnezzar was so furious with Shadrack, Meshach and Abednego that his face became distorted with rage. He commanded that the furnace be heated seven times hotter than before. Some of the strongest men in the army were ordered to bound Shadrach, Meshach and Abednego and throw them into the blazing furnace. They were meditating as this went on (Psalm. 23:3-6).

Shadrach, Meshach and Abednego were not threatened by the King's rage, nor perturbed by these strong army, nor mottled by the roaring of the blazing furnace, nor even terrified of the impending death, because of their understanding of the power of the unity they have with God, "Ye are of God, little children, and have overcome them because greater is he that is in you, than he that is in the world". (1John 4:4)

Could you ever imagine that only the flames from the burning furnace killed the soldiers as they threw Shadrach, Meshach and Abednego into the furnace?

The King Nebuchadnezzar was astonished with what he saw, that he called all his officials reminding them that he saw four men instead of three, unbound walking around in the fire unhurt.

"What shall we then say to these things? If God is for us, who can be against us? Romans 8:31, fear none of those things which you will suffer behold, the Devil shall cast some of you into prison, that you may be tried, and you shall have tribulation ten days, be faithful unto death and I will give you a crown of life". (Revelation 2:10)

Shadrach, Meshach and Abednego were able to travail and prevail over the circumstances of their lives through being resilient and having strong faith in God. Friend, the harder the enemy fights you, the harder you must fight to succeed. We accepted all these hurdles as marks of good fortune; sure enough the Devil had something he was fighting to protect and I was determined to fight and succeed in Jesus name (Luke 10:19).

When the Apostle Paul came to Corinth God gave him an assurance. Then spoke the Lord to Paul in the night by a vision, be not afraid but speak (Acts 18:9-10). God gave me a similar message concerning Maiduguri during a crusade. "My son be bold to preach my word. The tens of thousands who swarmed the crusade ground every night upset the forecasts of religious observers who believed that the programme was going to be a failure. But the first healing miracle testimony I received was that of a daughter of a leader of a Christian Organization which spread the news that God has a good sense in his movements.

At the end of our crusade, over two hundred men and women agreed to attend the bible school. I offered twenty full scholarships to the indigenes of Borno State for the session. Many had to be turned away due to lack of space and finance. To the glory of God, in the full glare of the skeptics and the doubting Thomas's, about three hundred converted Muslims and atheists were baptized into the body of Christ. Today the local Kanuris, Chiboks, Margis, Hausas and Shuwa-Arabs make up a vibrant assembly of believers in the Muslim city of Maiduguri. Friends, you can see how a man can overcome the circumstances militating against him and his ministry through faith and unity with God. Thus the course of the history of a state was changed by just understanding the power of unity with God.

We fail, when we have problems staring us FACE-TO-FACE, because we limit God by failing to understand and utilize the power of our unity with God. We can turn around our situations for the best just as Shadrach, Meshach and Abednego did when they were thrown into the burning furnace.

CHAPTER FOUR

The Power of Courage

We cannot write about understanding the power of unity with God without understanding the role of the power of courage, in enabling the power of unity with God to work in the life of a man in his walk with God. Let us examine from the scriptures, about the life of a man who the bible says is a **"man after God's own heart",** 1 Samuel 13-14.David was a shepherd; he spent long hours tendering his father's flock, playing music on his harp, meditating and praying to God .That experience alone with God forged an incredible and deep love of God in David's heart.

Our first example in the Bible of David's extraordinary understanding of God lies in one of the most famous stories about his life. His defeat of the giant Goliath was one.

"And there went out a champion out of the camp of the Philistines, named Goliath, of Gath, whose height was six cubits and a span. And he had a helmet of brass upon his head and he was armed with a coat of mail; and the weight of the coat was five thousand shekels of brass, and he had greaves of brass upon his legs and a target of brass between his shoulders. And the staff of his spear was like a weaver's beam, and his spears had weighed six hundred shekels of iron, and one bearing a shield went before hi. And he stood and cried unto the armies of Israel and said unto them, why are ye come out to set your battle in array/ am not a Philistine and ye servants to Saul? Choose you a man for you and let him come down to me, then will we be your servants; but if I prevail against him and kill him then shall ye be our servants, and serve us. And the Philistine said, I defy the armies of Israel this day give me a man, that we may fight together. When Saul and all Israel heard those words of the philistines they were dismayed and greatly afraid". 1 Samuel 17:4-11.

This giant Goliath was estimated to have stood about nine feet tall. His imposing figure and fearful countenance became a terror to the Israelites who cowered before him. Not even the best of their military lieutenants could stand the rage of the giant Goliath. But having looked at the logistical challenge that comes with facing such an imposing and overwhelming powerful foe, one young man looked deep into the supernatural with God and saw the reality – Goliath's challenges were against the supernatural God. He decided to walk with God to defeat the foe who terrorized God's own people.

"And David left his carriage in the hand of the keeper of the carriage and ran into the army and came and saluted his brethren, and as he talked with them, behold there came up the champion, the Philistine of Gath, Goliath by name out of the armies of the Philistines and spoke according to the same words and David heard them and all the men of Israel, when they saw the man, fled from him and were sore afraid, and the men of Israel said, have ye seen this man that is come up? Surely to defy Israel is he come up, and is shall be, that the man who killeth him the king will enrich him with great riches and will give him his daughter and make his father's house free in Israel. And David spoke to the men that stood by him saying, what shall be done to the man that killeth this Philistine, and taketh away the reproach from Israel for who is the uncircumcised Philistines, that he should defy the armies of the living God?"

1 Samuel 17:22-26.

David's question had nothing to do with doubting the Philistine's qualifications to wage battles; because there was no doubt that he was a well known warrior.

David was not interested in acquiring weapons sufficient enough to slay the giant, he understood through spiritual insight that the challenges of the Philistines were to be faced using the supernatural powers from God. And he sought the help of God through prayers. As it was written:

"You are of God, little children, and have overcome them because greater is he that is in you than he that is in the world", 1John 4:4.

He understood that the Philistine was not challenging the armies of Israel he was challenging their God.

"........Fear not, stand still and see the salvation of the lord which he will show to you today, for the enemies you see today, you shall see them again no more forever. The Lord shall fight for you and you shall hold your peace". Exodus 14:13-14.

In his mind it was impossible to believe that nobody had yet slain the giant in order to take the reproach away from Israel. How could it be that this uncircumcised Philistine giant had such enormous powers to defy the armies of the living God .Just as Jesus did when he saw the unbelief among his disciples, he was shocked and disappointed by their lack of faith. David found it hard to believe that there was no man in Israel who could face the insolent Philistine. This is another aspect of those who had the understanding of the power of unity with God; they understand that the Lord is a friend, who sticks closer than a brother. The Philistine's challenge had an underlying Spiritual cause- the Philistines had no respect for the God of Israel.

This is also the place where David demonstrated the character that was to make him Israel's greatest king. He was resilient to the treat of the famous arrogant Philistine giant. David was a courageous young man.

David, a mere boy, displayed a leadership skill that nobody in Israel had ever shown. He stepped up to grab that rare opportunity to lead the nation in both physical and spiritual exploits, as he accepted the challenge to face the giant. As he stepped out into the battle field David again demonstrated that he had a firm grasp of God's principles,

"And the Philistines said unto David, Am I a Dog that thou cometh to me with slings? and the Philistines cursed David by his gods and the Philistines said to David come to me and I will give thy flesh unto the fowl of the air and to the Philistine, thou cometh to me with a sword and with a spear and with a shield but I come to thee in the name of the Lord of Hosts, the God of the armies of Israel whom thou hast defied. This day will the Lord deliver thee into my hand and I will smote thee and take thy head from thee, and I will give the carcasses of the host off the Philistines this day unto the fowls of the earth may know that there is God on Israel. And all this assembly shall know that the Lord saveth not with sword and spear, for the battle is the Lord's and he will give you into our hands" 1Samuel 17:43-47.

David a mere boy understood the power of unity with God. He knew that no matter how many weapons of war the Philistines brought, he would not prevail against the God who did create the universe.

Although, David was faced with someone who could possibly be the hugest man he had ever seen, battle hardened and belligerent. David was not perturbed because he had faith in the God of his fathers.

All the mighty men of Israel were afraid of this massive man.

For David to face this immediate threat of death, he understood the power of unity. He had an absolute trust on the spiritual truths that he had learned while singing to the Lord and praying as he looked after his father's flocks.

"And it came to pass, when the Philistine arose and came and drew near to meet David and David hurried and ran towards the army to meet the Philistine. And David put his hand in his bag and took there a stone, slung it and struck the Philistine on his forehead, then the stone sunk into his forehead and he fell upon his face to the earth. So David prevailed over the Philistine with a sling and with a stone and struck the Philistine and slew him but there was no sword in the hand of David. Therefore David ran and stood upon the Philistine and took his sword and drew it out of its sheath and slew him and cut off his head there, and when the Philistines saw that their champion was dead they fled".

This is remarkable! So amazing!! This is understanding the power of unity with God in action as demonstrated by David.

But his prowess as a God-believing warrior was not the only aspect of David's character that showed the awesome power of God that was at work in him. A man can change the destiny of his nation, if he can believe God; believe in himself and with sheer determination to succeed where others have failed. If only men would turn their stumbling blocks into stepping stones, it would make all the difference.

When conditions became tough and unbearable for David, the bible says he **encouraged himself in the Lord**. That is what you should do in your difficult times. You should understand and believe that "the name of the lord is a strong tower; the righteous runneth into him and is safe". Proverb 18:10.

Sincerely understand that it is God who makes you to aspire to greater heights and He will give you the grace to succeed. Accept the fact that God has placed you on this earth to prevail and succeed "for in him we live and move and have our being……"Acts 17:28.

Aspiration is of man but the inspiration comes from God .One is externally generated, the other one is internally stimulated. God puts his desires for good into your heart when you are walking with Him, then will he give you the courage to conquer the foes.

CHAPTER FIVE

The Power of Discipline

One of the greatest men in the ancient world was the Patriarch Job. Some feel that he was a contemporary of Abraham, and therefore he lived on earth for about four hundred years before Moses. Some historians believe that he may have been the mastermind behind the construction of the Pyramids of Egypt.

In the early years of Job's life he was exceedingly blessed of God, among his assets were seven sons and three daughters, seven thousand sheep, three thousand camels, one thousand oxen, five hundred donkeys and a very great household no wonder the scripture says, "This was the greatest of all the men of the east".

Naturally Job had no problem with the pains and sorrows in those days, not with everything going well for him, but suddenly all that changed. His animals were stolen or slain and a tornado destroyed the home of his eldest son during a party, killing all his children. To make matters worse, his body was covered with boils. Although Job did not realize that he was being tested by God to prove his faithfulness to God, throughout all these tragedies he did not sin against God because of his love for God. He refused to run away from God, even when his wife encouraged him to curse God and die. Understanding the power of unity with God made him to remain positive despite the tragic events. Job's experiences would have plunged the average person into the pit of despair, but he did not allow himself to go down that route. This earned him the reputation of the world's most patient man.

Everyone have their own break up point and for him the final straw was when his three best friends came over to encourage him to confess the sin in his life that brought the tragedies. This great man was in great pain .Job understood God and this made him to maintain his discipline and patience with God. It also helped to lift his spirit up despite the tragedies; he then entered into a debate with his friends attesting to the faithfulness of God. Job's massive faith in God was apparent in Chapters 9 and 41 indicating that he understood the power of unity with God even before his circumstances changed as a result, God blessed Job with "twice as much as he had before" Job 4:10, not only were his riches restored, but he and his wife were given seven more sons and three beautiful daughters in addition to long life and health .He lived for one hundred and forty more years and saw four generations of his children.

Note this testimony;

I am a devoted Christian and an elder in the church. I am also a businessman, my business was moving smoothly and my family was very comfortable. One day my little daughter complained of weaknesses all over her body. I thought that it might be malaria or pains. A pharmacist prescribed some drugs for her and instead of her getting well, she became very weak. I became confused, each passing day and my only option was to trust God and pray for her. One day, I came back from work and was told that my little girl (6 years) was not able to walk .I could not believe it when I discovered that it was true. I mustered up courage and took her to hospital, the entire test was conducted and at last nothing was found and the doctor became tired. Everything became strange to me and I told devil that he was a liar. I started taking this little girl to all the specialist hospitals in Nigeria, but nothing changed. My business went down, because I had spent all my money seeking medical help for her. I bought new tyres, changed new oil and other things to make sure that I was able to meet the demand of having to move her around. There was no joy in family because of what we were passing through but I maintained my faith in God. One day, I heard that a great man of God was holding a crusade at Enugu; I took my little girl **(crippled)** and drove all the way from Kaduna to Enugu. When I got to Enugu, it was very late, so I decided to pass the night at my sister's house in preparation for the next day's crusade. When my sister saw the condition of my little girl, she wept bitterly she discouraged me from going to the crusade but rather suggested that I should see a witch doctor. I took my little girl in a rage and drove out of her house to the crusade ground believing that God is a miracle working God. When the crusade started, I left my little girl (crippled) in the custody of an elderly Christian mother. As the glory of God filled the place, my little girl opened a bible and said, "I see Jesus calling me come! Come!! She continued repeatedly and suddenly, she stood up and began to walk. This is a very wonderful testimony that came as a result of my having the understanding of how the power of unity with God works for those who believe. The scripture says; "with man it is impossible but with God all things are possible".

Understanding the Power of Unity with God does many things for you;

- It gives you directions in life
- It helps you to establish the right priorities in your life, family.
- It helps you to say "no" to the other voices that are calling for your attention.
- It energizes you to work with great energy because you ought to succeed.
- It helps you not to be jealous of other people's successes.
- It helps you to be contented with what you are doing.

Is the Lord with you? Moses said "if your presence does not go with us, do not send us up from here" Jesus said, "Surely, I am with you always" (Matthew 28:20). The last words that John Wesley said before he died were, "the best of all, God is with us". Life may not be easy, but if (God is with you) he will always make a way where there seems to be no way. When you know this life will be rich and rewarding for you if you walk at unity with God.

Job was able to see past the offences of his wife and three best friends to what God was really doing in his life. God wants us to do the same thing. Sometimes God allows bad things to come into our lives to give us direction or to prepare us for some promotions. We must not get so bogged down with the negative details of our day to day bad experiences that we fail to see the bigger picture of what God is doing in our lives. We must always remember Romans 8:28, "And we know that in all things God works for the good of those who love him, who have been called according to his purpose".

Now what is your attitude towards the negative circumstances of your life? Romans 8:35, "who shall separate us from the love of Christ? -Shall tribulation or distress or persecution, or famine, or nakedness, or peril, or sword".

To Job's great credit, he accepted all the negative experiences without becoming bitter or resentful towards God. These experiences got Job prepared to take up a greater position of power and influence.

His wife and his three best friends focused on the human offenses which they assumed that Job had committed. They had wanted Job to curse God and die. However, Job was focused on the bigger picture, he did not see the human offenses but what God wanted to accomplish through his tribulations. He knew that God was at work for his own good. That was a man who understood the power of unity with God at work in his own life.

God has a purpose even in the negative things that happen to us also. There may be further lessons of discipline that we need to learn so that God can bless our lives and families with his grace.

God wants us to focus more on the positive than the negative, the wise man said "yet man is born to trouble as surely as sparks fly upward" Job 5:7).

We would always have tribulations in this life; however, God is calling us not to focus on the bad things but on the good things. He is calling us to discipline our lives and not to worry so much about the negative things or circumstances. God wants us to focus more on the bigger pictures rather than the offences and inconveniences we might have experienced in life. This is what understanding the power of unity all is about.

What does it mean to be a disciplined person? A disciplined person is a person who not only refuses to do things that are wrong, but does all the right things expected of him or her, disciplined people are those who fulfill their goals, disciplined people always take responsibility for their actions.

Conclusion:

The primary lesson to learn from Job is not only that we must rejoice despite any unbelievably tragic circumstances, but also that even when we don't at first, it is still possible to gain only when we understand the power of unity with God by looking to God in faith. He is always faithful to his children, for he knows how much we can bear. Job was mightily used by God after his triumph over tragedy.

Generations who study the word of God learn through his experiences and he was mentioned among the heroes of faith.

CHAPTER SIX

The Power of Responsibility

Nehemiah was born in a foreign country and lived there until he returned to his home country. Although his family had been in Babylon for several generations, he was not an indigene of Babylon. His real home was back in Judea and no matter how many years he lived in Babylon, he never really would have fitted in because he was a non-indigene.

Nehemiah was an outstanding leader because of his understanding of the power of unity. Nehemiah was a wine taster in the Persian court of king Artaxerxes. He got word that the walls of Jerusalem were in serious despair. He prayed and asked God to help him and he got the answer to that problem. He later approached the king who gave him the permission to return to Jerusalem and rebuild the walls. He went back to Jerusalem and organized the walls of the city. He faced many different kinds of obstacles and problems but he persevered through them all and he was ultimately very successful in accomplishing his goal by understanding the power of unity.

Nehemiah was certainly born in exile. His family had been in this foreign land for at least five generations, perhaps as long as one fifty years, he was brought up in the Persian Empire, but his parents made him to understand that he was a Jew and belonged in Jerusalem. Jewish people had always considered Palestine to be their homeland.

Nehemiah 1:2 says; "Hanani one of my brothers came from Judah with some other men", the implication is that they came to report to him because they knew he would be interested in the condition of his people in Judah. Nehemiah wanted to know about his people so he asked questions, "And I questioned them about the Jewish remnant that survived the exile and also about Jerusalem.

After getting over the emotional reaction, Nehemiah prayed for his people and his home country, saying, "I said; O lord, God of Heaven...... (Nehemiah. 1:5-6). In other words, he came back to his senses.

Nehemiah taught us the importance of remembrance and getting homes, families, communities and countries to make peace, foster progress, be patriotic and take responsibilities through understanding the power of unity.

He did not abuse his privilege as a respectable person. He said, Nehemiah: 2:12: "Set out during the night with a few men". I had not told anyone what my God had put in my heart to do for Jerusalem! This shows that Nehemiah knew that there must be problems and obstacles and he cannot do it without understanding the Power of unity with God.

The residents of Jerusalem had become accustomed to broken walls. Nehemiah challenged them to do something about themselves. He used his experiences in Babylon to think about the situation back at home.

Our governments ought to embrace the importance of understanding the power of unity by encouraging our sons and daughters to contribute and invest back home.

Nehemiah knew that the king would be interested in helping to develop one of the cities that were under his control, by rebuilding the city of Jerusalem; Nehemiah actually helped the Persian government who controlled the city. Nehemiah had found a way to help the government and help his own cause well. That is called understanding the power of unity.

The world right now, is very concerned about the AIDS epidemic. So anyone who creates a plan that will help with the AIDS problem should get an approval for everyone to achieve the set goal.

Bruce Olsen's story is one of the most remarkable missionary sagas of the twentieth century. He moved into a group of head-hunting Indians in South America, it took some time but he eventually became accepted in South America. He wanted to help the people but he wanted to do so using their existing cultural and social structure for months, he tried to figure out a way to help with their medical problems. He brought in medicine and tried get people to take it, but they had absolute faith in the witch doctors. He knew that he could bypass the witch doctors and go directly to the people and give the results he needed but he remembered an important principle, "Take everyone with you". He knew that if he bypasses the witch doctors that he would reduce her reputation in the community and would make an enemy out of her. Finally, one day he saw a way out, there was an outbreak of pink eye in the village and everyone was miserable with the witch doctors. She tried all her incantations but nothing happened. Finally, Bruce rubbed his finger in the corner of someone's eyes and then rubbed this into his own eyes, in a couple of days he had a very good case of pink eye. He then went to the witch Doctor and asked her to rub a certain kind of antibiotic in his eyes. She had refused to do this before to her own people because this was white man's medicine. However she reluctantly agreed to rub this on his eyes. Within a few days he was well while everyone else was still miserable with her having success with him, he finally convinced her to try this medicine on someone. In a very short time, she was able to cure everyone in the village and she became recognized for what she did. She was now a learner from Bruce Olsen. Bruce had learned to take everyone with him and was able to influence the people by doing so. You can now see a very good example of understanding the power of unity as demonstrated by Bruce Olsen.

Nehemiah went back to Jerusalem, did his inspection and from the record of the people who participated in the rebuilding project, it was obvious that he took everyone with him. There are usually many people involved; for a project to be successful you must make all of the participants feel that they are part of the family, community, country, organization or project .There must be team spirit in our communities.

More so, Nehemiah could legitimately say that he was doing the king's work since king Artaxerxes had authorized it; it was no longer just a Jewish plan but also a Persian plan. When working with another person or organization, put the name of that person or organization in a prominent place. If the project is a joint project, promote the name of the other person, i.e. understanding the power of unity. He or she will like it and will help you to get the job done. Building Jerusalem's walls was a painful and difficult process that would have made a leader insignificant. Nehemiah however persisted in spite of the many difficulties that he had and he understood with God and king Artaxerxes .Unless you are patient and willing to continue praying and trying, you will not accomplish or prevail very much in life

Understanding the power of unity attracts quality character such as: integrity, honesty, righteous life and truth in the life of any person that possess it.

These were some of the qualities that attracted Nehemiah to the people with whom he would work.

"I put in charge of Jerusalem my brother Hanani alone with Hananiah the commander of the citadel, because he was a man of integrity and feared God more than most men do" (Nehemiah, 7:2).

Beloved you can now notice that understanding the power of unity gave them:

- ❖ Experience

- ❖ Construction
- ❖ Joy of improving their skill
- ❖ Opportunities to make decisions, correct and learn from their mistakes
- ❖ Joy of success

Without understanding the power of unity with God, the best plans, ideas or projects will fail. You have to work on the presentations and your relationship with people. Nehemiah began his career having a good relationship with the king. He took time before he approached the king with his idea of rebuilding the walls of Jerusalem. He knew that there would be an ideal time to approach the king, so, he waited. Nehemiah had good public relations skills, which is absolutely essential to be a successful person in life. He knew how important a good relationship was so he insisted on getting letters of safe passage and letters about the king's forests before he proceeded with the tasks. He even tried to maintain a cordial relationship with his enemies.

Sanballat was very angry when he learned that Nehemiah and his people were rebuilding the walls. He flew into a rage and mocked the Jews saying to his friends and the Samaritan army officers "what does this bunch of poor, feeble Jews think they are doing? Do they think they can build the wall in a day if they offer enough sacrifice? Look at those charred stones they are pulling out of the rubbish and are using them again".

Tobiah the Ammonite, who stood beside Sanballat, also said "that stone wall would collapse even if a fox walked along the top of it"

Nehemiah was not moved or distracted because he knew what understanding the power of unity with God meant, but when Sanballat and Tobiah, the Arabs, Ammonites and Ashodites heard that the work was going ahead and that the gaps in the wall were being repaired, they became furious. They all made plans to fight Jerusalem and to bring in confusion. They said "before they know what's happening we would swoop down on them and kill them and end their work."

Then, Nehemiah looked at the situation; he called together the leaders and the people and said to them, "Don't be afraid of the enemy! Remember the Lord who is great and Glorious, and fight for your friends, your families and your homes. They all prayed to God almighty and guarded the city day and night and protected themselves.

Then their enemies heard that they knew their plans and that God had frustrated them. Nehemiah and his people returned to their work on the walls.

You can note this remarkable victory as a result of understanding the power of unity with God as started by Nehemiah and his people.

One can have the smartest and best trained people or employees in the world, but if they are not interested or united in their work, the idea, plan or project will never be successful. Nehemiah had a sense of responsibility, which helped him to know how to motivate his people. How did Nehemiah motivate his people? He did so by conveying his vision by being a good example.

Remember, the best ideas, the best plans and the best money, cannot create success, unless there is an understanding of the power of unity with God in the life of a Christian. One of the most importance responsibilities that a leader has is to motivate people and make them feel good and be part of the family.

CONCLUSIONS

- Are you a responsible person?
- In which way are you motivating people?
- Do you pray for your family, community, country and organization?
- As a leader, are you willing to delegate authority?

CHAPTER SEVEN

The Power of Wisdom

Daniel was a young man when Jerusalem and Judah fell to the Babylonians.

One of Nebuchadnezzar's requirements for the defeated nation was for some of the young men from the royal families to come to Babylon and study for several years. They were to learn the Babylonian language, literature and culture .This would qualify them to become civil servants. As a result of this Daniel and his three friends were forced to leave their homeland and go to another land; where they became prisoners of war.

It would have been understandable if Daniel had become bitter and resentful toward his captor and had attempted to sabotage their plans for him. However, that was not what he was like, because of his background and understanding of the power of Unity with God, he had developed an excellent spirit (Proverbs. 3:5-7). Though there are many other ways through which Daniel demonstrated excellence in this foreign land.

There are five overlapping and notable phrases in Daniel 6:3-4. These are "distinguished himself" exceptional qualities, no corruption, trustworthy and neither corrupt nor negligent", all of these are the qualities that Daniel's phrase suggested which are very distinctive and should be part of everyone's character especially those who will **"Understand the Power of Unity".**

Firstly, Daniel "distinguished himself" and this was his hallmark, Daniel and his three friends were the top students in the Babylonian university. At the end of their courses, the king interviewed them and "found none equal to Daniel, Hananiah, Mishael and Azariah (Daniel 1:19). Because of their excellent examination results, they were appointed to the king's service (Daniel 1:19). As they began their work, they also distinguished themselves, not only were they the best students in the school, but the king found them to be ten times better than all the magicians in the entire kingdom (Daniel 1:20). Because, Daniel excelled in his work, particularly in the interpreting of dreams, "the king placed Daniel in a high position and made him ruler over the entire province of Babylon .He placed him to be in charge of all his wise men (Dan 2:48-49). Latter, when the Babylonians were overthrown by Darius, Daniel was so distinguished that the king asked Daniel to manage the affairs of the entire kingdom (Dan 6:3). All of these promotions were testimonies that Daniel had an excellent spirit. He was exemplary and did his work well.

In Daniel 6:3-4, Daniel was described as a person in whom there was no corruption and he was neither corrupt nor negligent. One of the basic components of a strong character is honesty. Honesty meant that one speaks the truth, lives the truth and refuses to compromise his or her integrity in any way. Christians must be known as people who do things excellently (honestly) since everything we do has the name of Jesus attached to it.

There are 27 individual references to bribery in the Bible, the first one could be found in Exodus. 23:8 "or not accept a bribe, for a bribe blinds those who see and twists the words of the righteous" God is a God of justice and since bribery perverts justice, God is opposed to all forms of bribery. No matter the pressure or circumstances may have found himself, an absolute essential rule is the "Panacea or the Antidote to solving problem in families, community Africa and world at large.

More so, not only was there no corruption found in Daniel there was also "no negligence". This phrase spoke of another aspect of his good character and that was the ability to take responsibility. Daniel did his job so well that two things happened. Firstly, he was noticed by his superiors as being gifted with the ability to do excellent work. People always think that the reward for excellent service is often more work, but in this case he was promoted.

Secondly, he was noticed by his colleagues, the high standard of his work kept them uncomfortable; Daniel's diligence made them somehow look incompetent and hindered their own possibilities of advancement.

You should be examples of excellence, even if you are surrounded with problems or given assignments you do not like, do it with all of your heart (Colossians . 3:23) as unto the Lord (Col. 3:17) only with wisdom. The story of Daniel provides us with a model character. One of the most obvious characteristics of a man with an excellent spirit is wisdom. Knowledge is the accumulation of information. Wisdom is knowing how to use the information, a successful person in life is one who is excellent in his spirit , wisdom is not something that you are born with or even can learn in school, wisdom starts with the fear of the Lord (Psalm 111:10) and it grows with experience.

One of the most important characteristics of a Christian who had understood the power of unity is having the ability to relate to others (Daniel 6:3) says," Now Daniel so distinguished himself among the administrators by his exceptional qualities that the king planned to set him over the whole kingdom, at least one of those exceptional qualities was his outstanding ability to get along with other people .Romans 12:18 says, "If it is possible, as far as it is depends on you, live at peace with everyone", this is a good description of Daniel's life in Babylon. In his understanding of the power of unity with God Daniel tried very hard to get along with everyone in Babylon.Anyone living and co-existing with others in the different fields of life will always have superiors. There are government officials, community leaders, church officials, and leaders from different organizations -that we must relate with.

This is an age of uncertainty; depression and fear .There are men and women who fear everything. More than ever before, men are plagued by the spirit of fear. For some hope is lost, countless millions are looking for refuge in something, provided it can offer a shadow of consolation for a moment of time, but inflation, depression, wars, corruption, poverty, come too soon and sweep all hope away. The whole world is looking for the solution to human problems and it is only when a man becomes united with his creator, would they become partners in bringing down his glory on earth. Daniel gave us a positive example of how to relate with all these. Daniel was a source of inspiration and a challenge to his friends and the others he worked with. Daniel and his friends clearly stood for principles. His immediate superior decided that Daniel and his friends should eat the food provided by the king. Note what happened in Daniel 1:8 "But Daniel resolved not to defile himself with the royal food and wine and he asked the chief official for permission not to defile himself this way". Daniel purported in his mind in other words, he made up his mind. This is having an understanding of the purpose of God in action. The question now is, how do you react when you are faced with the challenges or problems of life? Do you reason in unity with God? Daniel knew that what he was being asked to do was a big problem to him and his friends, but Daniel and his friends made up their minds in one spirit to be in one purpose with God, and Daniel said , "Please test your servants for ten days", (Daniel. 1:12). "Then let our countenance be looked upon before you, and the countenance of the young men that eat of the portion of the king's food and as you see fit, deal with your servants", (Daniel 1:13). What a statement full of confidence showing and understanding the power of unity with God. At the end of their course, "And the king spoke with them and among them all was found none like Daniel, Hananiah, Mishael and Azariah therefore stood they before the king, and in all matters of wisdom and understanding, that the king inquired of them and found them ten times better than all the magicians and astrologers that were in all his realms", you can see with me how understanding the power of unity was demonstrated by Daniel and his friends in Babylon. Daniel was appointed to the king's service even though they were sojourners in the land after he overcame the challenge of being thrown into the lion's den through faith in the almighty God.

Dairus latter worshipped the God of Daniel and commanded his people to offer sacrifices and burnt sweet incense before him. Daniel climbed the ladder of success until he was the number three person in the whole Persian Empire. Note what happened in this story –As Daniel climbed the ladder of success by distinguishing himself among the administrators and princes through his exceptional qualities, he created enemies who attempted to pull him down but they couldn't find anything against him. They promulgated a law against his religion. When Daniel learned that the law was signed, he went home and knelt down as usual in his room, with its window open towards Jerusalem. He prayed three times a day, just as he had always done giving thanks to his God .Daniel was not moved neither was he troubled because of his understanding of the power of unity with the almighty God.

On hearing it, the king was very angry with himself for signing the law and he tried to find a way to save Daniel. He spent the rest of the day looking for a way to get Daniel out of the predicament. At last Daniel was arrested and thrown into the Lion's Den. Then, the king returned to his usual entertainment and couldn't sleep that night.

Very early the next morning, the king hurried out to the Lion's Den and called out Daniel in pity, saying; "Daniel servant of the Living God! Was your God whom you whom worship continually, able to deliver you from the lions? Daniel answered; "My God sent his angel to shut the Lion's mouths so that they would not hurt me, for I have found favour in his sight". Then the King was overjoyed and ordered that Daniel be lifted from the Den and not a scratch was found on him. "Those that know their God shall be strong and do great things" (Dan 11:32). Notice this, first Daniel found favour before the king. Secondly, Daniel found favour before the living God. As it is written, "And Jesus increased in Wisdom and Stature and in favour with God and Man" (LK 3:5). So Daniel prospered during the reign of Darius and the reign of Cyrus the Persians. Daniel gave a very remarkable example of understanding power of unity. **Conclusion:**

- Would people around you say that you have an excellent character?
- Do you develop and maintain an excellent relationship with God?
- Are you characterized by excellence in wisdom?

CHAPTER EIGHT

The Power of Working with God

Moses was actually born in a foreign country, although his people had been in Egypt for almost four hundred years, they were never accepted and continued to be "foreigners" even after living for so many years in the land. On the other hand, Moses had an unusual experience, though his parents were Israelites, he was actually raised in Pharaoh's palace. Since Moses was a young child when he went to the palace, it was unlikely that he remembered many details about his Jewish roots later on in life. Moses lived in Pharaoh's court during the first forty years of his life.

Because Moses was adopted by Pharaoh's daughter, he was brought up in luxury. He lived in a palace; he had everything he could possibly have wanted including the best clothes, good food and servant to make life easy for him. Egypt had the ideal climate throughout his youthful years; he was comfortable and lacked nothing. In Egypt, Moses had lived with the Elite. He was accustomed to having royal visitors and the best available entertainment.

Yet Moses had a big problem, he was greatly burdened by the desire to help his people to move out of the bondage of Egypt and its Pharoah.Eventually this moved him and when God saw his heart, He called him and opened his eyes on the importance of "Understanding the Power of Unity", God did not want him to walk "ALONE" but to walk with him to achieve the purpose of delivering His own people.

Thus "Also I heard the voice of the Lord saying, whom shall I send and who will go for us?" Then I said, "Here am I send me".

When Moses was in the desert, God began to prepare him for the task ahead. God spoke to him from a burning bush .He threw his rod on the ground which later turned to a snake to show the power of the almighty God. When Moses got back to Egypt, God used him to perform many other miracles. His rod became a snake and swallowed the Egyptian Pharaohs' snake. He was able to turn the river into blood. He was able to send frogs and insects and other things to afflict the Egyptians and force Pharaohs' hand to move. This he did through faith and an having **"Understanding the Power of God"** (Assistance of God Almighty).

The miracles performed by God through Moses did not stop there. The greatest miracle in the Old Testament was the crossing of the Red sea. This was an absolutely amazing miracle. This is the miracle that is constantly referred to as a true demonstration that God was with him.

That was not the end of the miracles, however God miraculously provided quail for the people to eat and water out of a rock. God caused manna to come down from the heaven for the entire forty years the Israelites through the desert. God miraculous led the Israelite through the desert by a cloud in the daytime and fire at night. On one occasion the ground opened and swallowed some people who were attempting to stage a rebellion. All of these were supernatural demonstrations that God was with Moses because he had an understanding of the Power of Unity at work with God.

We are serving the same God that Moses was serving. You are doing God's will just as much as Moses was doing God's will in those days. God has lost none of his supernatural power and is just as capable of doing supernatural things today as he was in those days.

The big question then is where is the supernatural in our lives? Many Christians today are caught up in the wave of the "artificial" miracles. The answer to life's issues is simply walking with God while having an understanding of what the power of unity with Him can do.

Moses was raised in the Pharaoh's Egyptian palace as Egypt was one of the most advanced countries in the world at that time. He had so many opportunities to enjoy himself. He had the best training even as a military officer in the Egyptian Army. Moses did not yield to that temptation. He preferred to live the same kind of life and conditions of the common people in order to deliver and set this people free and fulfill his purpose of God check out this Excerpt;

One singular event took place in the life and ministry of one of the ministers of God that I respect most Archbishop Benson Idahosa of the Blessed memory which had a remarkable impact and effect on his faith and success. The short time he spent in Christ for the Nations Dallas, USA, in 1972 opened his eyes to the new faith and ministry that he was ready to launch into the deep for a bumper harvest of souls. In few years, a deep and lasting relationship between his family and the Osborn (Drs T.L and Daisy Osborn) was established.

Benson Idahosa said and I quote;" I have always revealed to people my gratitude and appreciation for the spiritual influence of the Osborne's upon my ministry. They mean everything to my family and little wonder I named one of my daughters 'Daisy' after that precious woman of God, the wife of Dr T.L Osborn. The Osborn's took us into their confidence sharing secrets of apostolic evangelism and ministry with us. In November, 1975 ,we accepted an invitation to visit them in Tunisia. For us it was a historic visit. More than that, it was a life-changing journey in my adventure of faith. Above all, it was a mission which helped to prove God beyond measure.

It was a fabulous experience to be special guests to the Osborn's. We were overwhelmed by the goodness of God upon them, a remarkable evidence of the honour and reward for their faithful service in his kingdom. Great ministerial opportunities and new doors opened before us by through the Osborn's. Preaching engagements flooded my desk from the United States of America. A new era of fruitful ministry stood before us like on open door. It was a challenge and bait!

During a couple of weeks stay in the United States of America, Dr Osborn tapped on my door to discuss a very crucial issue with me. "Dear Benson" he said, I have a rather important issue to discuss with you" I ushered him to a sofa in the corner, What is it Brother Osborn? I enquired smiling into his ever cheerful face, Benson he began; I want you to consider the offer of ministerial appointment here in U.S.A. "You will be offered not less than fifteen hundred dollars a month for pastoral duties".

I was so overwhelmed by the proposal that I momentarily lost my power of speech. I sat there staring at Dr. Osborne, who gripped my hands in assurance. Then the Osborn's took us both for a ride through the sprawling city. Down the smooth, well-kept road we drove in luxury. As we negotiated a curve, Dr Osborn reiterated lovingly, "My Dear Benson, you are most welcome to live here with us if you so desire; be free to think about it with Margaret.

The neat mown lawns and beautiful setting of the city as we sped by caught my attention, under my breath I sighed; a city of splendor and. Dr. Osborn's attractive proposal did not put me at ease. I invited Margaret to help me examine the full spectrum of this great offer. "This is a dream come true!!!" She exclaimed delightedly; honey with your growing anointed ministry we can believe God for new horizons of exploits for the kingdom here in America.

My mind was confused. I was standing at cross roads, no decision had tested my faith like this new development and of course I knew the implications.

My thought reeled back to Benin City, Nigeria. The contrast was sharp and vivid. An emerging ministry there was going through deep-sealed trials. In the background was the city of blood (Benin) yielding easily to the gospel. Everything at home pointed to a promising ministry, but down in my heart, I knew it was going to be a long way to victory.

Suddenly I thought of the meager salary, I was receiving in Nigeria as pastor-evangelist, the equivalent of fifteen U.S Dollars a month. What was fifteen Dollars in Nigeria in the U.S.?

The time for fervent prayers has come; I did not need anyone to tell me that. I called Margaret "Honey Please let us seek the face of God on this crucial issue. I want us to walk in the perfect will of God, Whatever the cost is"

Together in earnest prayers we called upon the Lord for his divine directions. I went to bed with mixed feelings about the issue, subject to divine overruling over our decisions. I intended to go with Dr. Osborn's offer – or so? .I think that day we went to bed in high spirits.

At midnight, I felt someone touch me; I went down on my knees in agonizing prayers. The presence of the Lord filled the room. My wife was in deep sleep, and the Lord spoke clearly to me. He left me in no doubt concerning what he wanted to communicate to me. There was no room for guess work with God, and his words are straight and emphatic.

The Lord insisted; "Benson, go back to Nigeria that is where I had called you to be, if you stay in America I will kill you".

In a twinkle of an eye I saw the dream fizzle out into the thin air and there I lay before the Lord on the floor. What seemed a chance of a life time evaporated before my eyes, fear seized me and there was no more strength left in a momentary meditation I gently said, "O Lord God, why, why? Then in the haziness of my mind I heard the Spirit of God saying words I shall never forget all the days of my life. Words that have changed my life, my vision and above all ministry, God said, my Dear son Benson, go back to Africa. I called you as my vessel from there to the rest of the world. Whatever things you desire, as long as you preach my words of salvation, healing and power, I shall provide all. Go back now!!

After a prayer of thanks I bounced to my feet with renewed vigour and strength. I buttoned up my shirt and headed for Dr. Osborn's apartment. The clock sounded 2:00am. I knocked firmly and when Dr. Osborn came to the door I said calmly to him, "Please, Dr. Osborn, God spoke to me. I cannot accept the offer, I must go back home. For moments not one more word was uttered between us, then with a deep, sincere smile Dr. Osborn placed his hands on my shoulder an assured me, thank you, Benson, goodnight and God bless you. Great men of God honour his word!

Before long Margaret and I were on a plane back to Nigeria, we have seen rough and bitter moments since then. There have been times when there seemed to be no light at the end of the tunnel, but the words of Jesus reassured me, "have faith in God (Mark 11:22) (Proverbs. 3:5-7).

With divine precision the Almighty God has blessed us beyond measure in the ministry. I have witnessed overwhelming growth and in my family God's word have come true, "The blessing of the Lord it maketh rich and addeth no sorrow with it".

Beloved friend, do not look on the prevailing circumstances, but depend on the power that comes with having an understanding of working at Unity with God.

Moses poured his life into other people; he did not walk in isolation nor had he any personal agenda in his walk with God. All the works Moses did in Egypt was at unity with God to deliver his people from the slavery of Egypt and to set them free from the tyranny of Pharaoh. He worked with the leadership team made up of Aaron and Miriam. Aaron his spokesman was mentioned two hundred and sixty three times and Miriam the (Woman leader) ten times in the Pentateuch. These were the primary leaders that worked with Moses to accomplish his goal. Consequently, he spent lots of time with them when Joshua successfully completed the military campaign and defeated the Amelekites in which Moses hands were held up (Exodus 17:9-13), it became very obvious that they had an understanding of the power of Unity and it worked for them (Moses, Aaron, Hur and Joshua).

CHAPTER NINE

The Power of Commitment

Joseph was the eleventh son of Jacob, but was the first son of his favourite wife and was born after many years of barrenness. Joseph became the favorite son of his father. Joseph's brothers resented him and that caused problems between them. When Joseph was seventeen years old, he had two dreams. In the first dream the members of the family were binding sheaves. The sheaves of his brothers and sisters and parents came and bowed down to his sheaf (Genesis 37:5-7). In the second dream, the sun and moon and stars came and bowed down to him (Genesis. 37:9). When Joseph shared these dreams with his family, this created even more jealousy and resentment towards Joseph.

Joseph fulfilled the will of God for his life because he understood the power of unity with God. How did God lead Joseph to the point that he was able to fulfill God's will for his life? Although it was not as dramatic nor was there as much direct contact between God and Joseph as there had been between God and Abraham, Joseph committed himself to God and was led one step at a time.

Joseph went to look for his brothers in obedience to his father, this action led to him being sold into Egypt when his brothers conspired against him. This was how he became a slave in Potipha's house. Joseph committed himself to God and was faithful while he worked in Potipha's house. One day when everyone else was gone from the house, Potipha's wife attempted to get Joseph to commit adultery with her. When he refused, the woman began to shout and accused him of attempting to rape her. When Potipha heard about this he put Joseph in prison. Joseph who understood the power of unity committed himself to God. Look at what he said to Potipha's wife;

"There is nothing greater in the house than I, neither has he kept back anything from me but you, because you are his wife, how then can I do this great wickedness and sin against God?"

Joseph was jailed for life, while he was in prison two prisoners had dreams. Joseph was able to correctly interpret the dreams, one of the prisoners was released and went back to serve the king. About two years later, Pharaoh had a dream, the king's cupbearer who had been in prison remembered that Joseph had correctly interpreted his own dream and informed Pharaoh. Pharaoh sent for Joseph and told him his dream and Joseph was able to correctly interpret it. The dream predicted seven years of abundance and the seven years of drought that were to come upon the land. Pharaoh was so impressed that he said; unto his servants; "can we find such a one, as this is a man in whom the Spirit of God is"? Since God has showed Joseph all these there is none as discreet and wise as he. He shall be over my house and according unto his word shall all my people be ruled, only in the throne will I be greater than Joseph" (Genesis 41:38-40). And Pharaoh said unto Joseph; see, I have set you over all the land of Egypt (Genesis. 41:41). Oh! What a strong great word of fulfillment!! Pharaoh took off his own signet ring from his hand and put it upon Joseph and arrayed him in clothing of fine linen, and put a gold chain about neck.

Joseph fulfilled all Pharaoh's expectations, organized the nation very well and stored food in preparation for the famine.

Joseph was able to fulfill his destiny and dream as a result of his (commitment) and having an understanding of the power of unity with God.

Amazingly every aspect of the story was important in helping Joseph to locate his destiny. In our contemporary families especially in Africa we have extended families. We always find jealousy, strife and resentment among brothers, sisters, uncles and aunties over any person (child) that has a very bright future (destiny).Many start to fight children's destinies from birth. Hence the reason why there is no prosperity in some families. "Knowing their thoughts, he told them every kingdom divided against itself falls" (Luke 11:17).

You can now see with me that;

Unity is Progress
Unity is Peace
Unity is Strength
Unity is Success
Unity is Prosperity
Unity is Joy, Happiness and Blessing
Unity is Love, Forgiveness, Purpose, Power etc.

NOTE: GOD PREPARED JOSEPH FOR THE IMPORTANT POSITION THAT HE WAS TO OCCUPY THROUGH DIFFICULT CIRCUMSTANCES:

Doing God's will is the best thing for us but it is not always the easiest thing to do, did Joseph do the will of God? Yes, he certainly did, simply because, he understood the power of unity with God ,but he went through difficult times which most of us would never want to go through , it is always best to do the will of God but the path of God's will is often difficult and painful.

Now see this excerpt about the life of **Chuck Colsen**;

Chuck Colsen was the personal advisor to the president of the United States of America with an office in the white house, he found himself caught up in the Watergate Scandal. During this time, he became a committed believer, unfortunately, though he tried everything he could to avoid it, but he eventually went to prison for his Watergate crimes. It was during his time in prison that he trusted and committed himself more to Understanding Power of unity with God, and afterwards, God helped him to establish the largest prison ministry in the world.

Chuck Colsen never would have created **Prison fellowship International**, if he did not go through the embarrassing and painful experience of going to prison himself.

There are many lessons that we can learn from Joseph's life. However, Joseph understood what the Power of Unity with God can do in the life of a man which made him to believe in the sovereignty of God,

As it is written;

"And we know that all things work together for good to them that love God, to them who are the called according to his purpose" (Rom. 8:28). What is your attitude towards the negative happenings in your life? Can you see that God may be doing something bigger than you can imagine? Sometimes God allows bad things to come into our lives to give us directions or to prepare us for our lives and destiny.

NEGATIVE EXPERIENCES AS OPPORTUNITIES:

We all want to be successful in what we do; Joseph undoubtedly was one of the most successful people in the Old Testament.

Joseph's life was filled with many negative experiences especially in the early stages. He was betrayed by his brothers, he was sold into slavery, he was falsely accused by his master's wife, he was thrown into prison, and he was forgotten by the people he had helped. However, in all these circumstances Joseph never allowed himself to get bitter, he simply did the best that he could and trusted God to work all these things out for his own good.

CONCLUSION:

The book of Genesis records and revealed to us the real secrets behind Joseph's successes. This could be found in three simple verses:

- Genesis. 39:2 – "The Lord was with Joseph and he prospered"
- Genesis. 39:20-21 – "But while Joseph was there in prison, the Lord was with him, he showed him kindness and gave him favour in the sight of the prison warden"
- Genesis. 41:38 – "So Pharaoh asked them, can we find anyone like this man, one in whom is the Spirit of God?"

What does this verse teach us?

Simply put, Joseph Understood and utilized the Power of Unity with God in all his dealings with men. He was a man who sought God in every situation.

CHAPTER TEN

The Power of Obedience

Abraham's father, Terah, had three sons and lived at Ur of the Chaldeans. When one of his sons died, Terah decided to migrate with his son Abraham and other members of his family to the northwest beside the Euphrates River. Terah chose to settle in an area called Haram which was located northwest of the area that we now call Palestine.

Even before Terah and his family left Ur, the Lord spoke to Abram and said 'Leave your country, your people and your father's household and go to the land I will show you' (Genesis. 12:1). In going with his father to Haram, Abraham began an act of obedience to the word that the Lord gave to him while he was still in Ur.

After his father Terah died, Abraham continued his journey from Haram with his nephew Lot and headed southwest into Canaan or Palestine. The Lord promised that he would make a mighty nation out of Abraham and that eventually all the people of the earth would be blessed through him (Genesis. 12:2-3). They appeared to him near Bethel and told him that he was going to give this land to his descendants. Abraham then made a short trip down into Egypt and the Lord blessed him richly with wealth as a result of obedience, but later returned to the land of Canaan.

The Lord appeared to Abraham again and assured him that a son could come from your own body who will be your heir (Genesis 15:4) Sarah believed the message the Lord gave to her husband, but she was beyond the normal child bearing age, so the Lord appeared to Abraham again and told him that his wife, Sarah would have a son who would be the fulfillment of God's promise. Isaac was later born when Abraham was one hundred years "(As it is written, I have made you a father of many nations, before him whom he believed even God, who gives life to the dead and calls those things which are not as though they were. Who against hope believed in hope, that he might become the father of many nations according to that which was spoken, so shall your descendant be. And being not weak in faith, he considered not his own body as now dead, when he was about a hundred years old, neither yet the deadness of Sarah's womb. He staggered not at the promise of God. And being fully persuaded that what he had promised he was able also to perform".

It is not only important to be a Christian, it is also important to have some understanding about God's relationship and its power at work in your life. In other words, the more intimate the relationship you have with God the more successful you are likely to be in life. Here are some examples;

Moses understood God's purpose for him that he will be the one to lead the people out of Egypt and help them to establish a relationship with God.

Joshua understood God's purpose that he will be the one to conquer the land Canaan and direct them towards God.

David understood God's purpose for him that as a King over Israel he was to be a leader who will direct his nation towards God.

Nehemiah understood God's purpose for him that he will be the leader who would rebuild the wall of Jerusalem and help his people to establish a relationship with God.

Paul understood God's purpose for him to be an apostle to the Gentiles and help people to establish good relationship with God.

MAINTAINING A PERSONAL RELATIONSHIP WITH GOD

One of the most wonderful things about Abraham was that he maintained a close (intimate) personal relationship with the Lord. Abraham had apparently met the Lord in Ur of the Chaldeans. Over the years his relationship with God did not die or grow stale. He continued to have an ongoing relationship with God throughout his life.

Note these Incidents:

- Genesis. 12:7 – (After Abraham arrived in Canaan): The Lord appeared to Abraham and said, "To your offspring I will give this land"
- Genesis. 13:14-17 – (After Lot had left Abraham): The Lord said to Abraham after Lot had parted from him, lift up your eyes from where you are and look North ,South East and West. All the land that you see? I will give to you and you're off springs forever. I will make your offspring like the dust of the earth, so that if anyone could count the dust, then your offspring could be counted go walk through the length and breadth of the land for I am giving it to you."
- Genesis. 15:1 – (After this, the word of the Lord came to Abraham in a vision): do not be afraid, Abraham, I am your shield, your very great reward". It was at this time that the Lord told Abraham that his servant would not be his heir but "a son would come from your own body who will be your heir" Genesis. 15:4. It was also in conjunction with this appearance that the Lord called for the sacrifice of a heifer, a goat, a ram, a dove, and a young pigeon. These were sacrificed and their blood was used to establish a covenant with Abraham forever.
- Genesis. 17:1-2 "When Abraham was ninety nine years old, the Lord appeared to him and said, I am God Almighty; walk before me and be

blameless. I will confirm my covenant between me and you and will greatly increase your numbers". It was at this time that the Lord changed his name from Abram to Abraham; he had established a covenant with Abraham that would last forever. This was also when the Lord asked Abraham to be circumcised as a symbol of the covenant he had with God.

- Genesis. 18:1 The Lord appeared as a visitor to Abraham and confirmed that Sarah was going to have a baby. It was during this same visit that the Lord told Abraham that he was going to destroy Sodom and Gomorrah.
- Genesis. 21:12 – (After the conflict between Sarah and Hagar): "But God said to him, do not be so distressed about the boy and your maidservant. Listen to whatsoever Sarah tells you, because it is through Isaac that your offspring will be reckoned. I will make the son of the maidservant into a nation, also because he is your offspring".
- Genesis. 22:1 – This section described the time when the Lord told Abraham to sacrifice Isaac, at mount Moriah. Abraham obeyed even though it was very painful, after the Lord stopped Abraham from killing his son, he said (Genesis. 22:12), "Now I know that you do fear God, because you have not withheld from me your son, your only son".

In addition to the first time when God appeared to Abraham in Ur of Chaldeans, the Lord appeared to Abraham at least seven other times. James 2:23 says; Abraham believed God, and it was credited to him as righteousness and he was called God's friend. All of these suggest that Abraham not only had a relationship with the lord in Ur but he also maintained that relationship after he got to Canaan.

It is very easy to be a Christian and not have a close relationship with God. It is one thing to work for the lord. It is another to be a "friend of God" (intimate relationship) and have a close walk with Him. God wants our friendship more than he wants our work. How do we maintain that intimate relationship with God? We can do this by spending time communing with him in prayers. It is very vital to take notes as you have your quiet time and listen to God speak to you.

Go to church regularly and hear the word of God, spend time in bible study and prayer with other Christians. Make it one of your most vital goals in life to have an intimate relationship with God;

Now the questions are:

- Are you a friend of God like Abraham?
- Do you have an intimate relationship with God?
- Are you willing to make sacrifices?
- Do you have the determination to persevere in tough times?
- Are you maintaining a personal intimate relationship with God?

God has better plans for us so that together with Him these plans would be made perfect. Unless we maintain the unity of spirit with Him we are bound to fail in our assignment to bring His glory down on earth

Shalom

Prince .A. Onyechere 2015

9780993130892
BV - #0046 - 270420 - C0 - 210/148/4 - PB - 9780993130892